Guidelines

We have produced this workbook for junior high school and high school students using the North American Third Edition of the Cambridge Latin Course. The workbook adds reinforcement exercises to those already contained in the textbook. Because the exercises are supplementary and optional, students should work them after they have completed both the stories and the "Practicing the Language" drills in the textbook.

If students, while working the exercises, do not recognize the ending of an inflected Latin word or are puzzled by the structure of a Latin sentence, they should consult the relevant section in the "Review Grammar" of the Unit 1 textbook, pp. 202-12. If they do not know the English meaning of a Latin word, they should look up the Latin word in the "Complete Vocabulary" part of the Unit 1 textbook, pp. 213-21.

The "Progress Checks," one at the end of every three stages in the workbook, are meant to be rough indicators of a student's grasp of the relevant grammar, not exact measures of his or her total achievement. The teacher will find other, longer diagnostic tests in the Unit 1 Teacher's Manual, pp. 110-13, and may order Unit 1 achievement examinations from the Resource Center, North American Cambridge Classics Project (NACCP), Box 932, Amherst, MA 01004-0932 U.S.A.

Stage 1

1.1 What is he or she doing?

Circle the Latin verb in brackets which describes the action of the character in each picture.

1 Metella in ātriō (surgit / sedet).

2 Quintus in triclīniō (bibit / labōrat).

3 Caecilius in tablīnō (dormit / scrībit).

1.2 quid est nōmen? What is his name?

Write the correct name in each blank.

1   . . . . . in culīnā labōrat. . . . . . est coquus.
quid est nōmen?   _____

2   . . . . . in viā dormit. . . . . . est canis.
quid est nōmen?   _____

3   . . . . . in hortō labōrat. . . . . . est servus.
quid est nōmen?   _____

1.3 What does he say? What does he do?

Find the answer to each question by filling the blanks with Latin words which translate the English. Then read the boxed letters down.

1   quid Grumiō dīcit? What does Grumio say?

father

goes out

on the table

in the study

son

writes

2   quid Cerberus agit? What does Cerberus do?

works

stands

snores

enters

shouts

in the garden

1.4 Roman Houses

Not far from Pompeii is another ancient town called Herculaneum. Nearby, a lavish country house known as the Villa of the Papyri was partially excavated. This house has been recreated as the Getty Museum in Malibu, California. Part of it is shown in the photograph below.

Look carefully at the photograph, and compare it with the illustrations in your textbook, pp. 14 and 15, which show a typical Pompeian townhouse.

1   Point out which of the features of a Pompeian house listed below can also be seen in the photograph of the American museum above:

peristȳlium	larārium
ātrium	triclīnium
statua	hortus

2   Can you also point out some features in the photograph which are different from those in the illustrations of a Pompeian house? Can you suggest reasons for the differences?

Stage 2

2.1 Who does the action? Who or what receives it?

1 In each of the Latin sentences below, draw <u>one</u> line under the <u>nominative</u> and <u>two</u> lines under the <u>accusative</u>.

A   *Translation*

1 Grumiō triclīnium intrat.   _____

2 Grumiō pāvōnem portat.   _____

3 Metella pāvōnem gustat.   _____

4 pāvō Metellam dēlectat.   _____

5 Caecilius quoque pāvōnem gustat.   _____

6 pāvō Caecilium nōn dēlectat.   _____

B

1 Clēmēns triclīnium intrat.   _____

2 Clēmēns vīnum portat.   _____

3 Grumiō vīnum in mēnsā videt.   _____

4 coquus vīnum bibit.   _____

5 Caecilius Clēmentem vituperat.   _____

6 Clēmēns Grumiōnem vituperat.   _____

2 Write a translation for each sentence above in the spaces provided.

3 Compare your translations with the Latin sentences.
What is normally the position of the accusative in the English sentence?
In the Latin sentence?

2.2 Which answers are possible?

1 quid Metella gustat?
What does Metella taste?

Circle things Metella would enjoy tasting:

canem
culīnam
pecūniam
cēnam
hortum
pāvōnem
coquum

2 quem Clēmēns salūtat?
Whom does Clemens greet?

Circle only people:

amīcum
mēnsam
vīllam
mercātōrem
Quīntum
hortum
servum
ancillam
pāvōnem

3 quod conclāve Cerberus intrat?
Which room does Cerberus enter?

Circle only rooms:

ātrium
tablīnum
impluvium
cibum
triclīnium
culīnam
lectum
ancillam
vīnum
cubiculum

4 quid Metella agit?
What does Metella do?

Circle actions appropriate for Metella:

salit
dormit
sedet
clāmat
vīsitat
cēnat
stertit
gustat

Continued

5 quem Metella audit?
Whom does Metella hear?

Circle only animals or people:

fīlium
hortum
mēnsam
canem
coquum
pāvōnem
cēnam

6 quid Caecilius agit?
What does Caecilius do?

Circle actions appropriate for Caecilius:

scrībit
sedet
pecūniam numerat
lātrat
in lectō recumbit
salit
cantat
coquit

2.3 Find the hidden sentence

1 In this group, cross out every word describing a person. Read what remains.

māter   coquus   canis   fīlius   servus   pater   argentārius
in impluviō   ancilla   dominus   stat.

2 In this group, cross out every word describing movement. Read what remains.

salit   pater   surgit   exit   coquum   portat   vīsitat
vituperat   intrat.

3 In this group, cross out every accusative noun. Read what remains.

cibum   culīnam   canis   amīcum   servum   pāvōnem
ancillam   mercātōrem   est   pecūniam   pestis   iānuam
fīlium.

2.4 Cerberus

1 Fill in the missing Latin word which matches the English or the picture. You will not use all the items in the lists.

Nominative Nouns	Accusative Nouns	Verbs
Caecilius	Caecilium	clāmat
canis	canem	est
cēna	cēnam	exit
Cerberus	Cerberum	gustat
coquus	coquum	intrat
culīna	culīnam	laudat
dominus	dominum	parat
Grumiō	Grumiōnem	stat
servus	servum	videt

_____ est in culīna. coquus _____ parat. Caecilius
                                              (dinner)

culīnam _____ . _____ cibum gustat. Caecilius _____
              (enters)   (The master)   (the cook)

laudat. Cerberus _____ intrat. _____ cibum videt.
                      (the kitchen)

_____ cibum gustat. Grumiō _____ videt. _____
   (The dog)   (the dog)   (The slave)

nōn est laetus. "pestis!" _____ clāmat. _____
                                (the cook)

est īrātus. "furcifer!" dominus _____ . Cerberus exit.
                                     (shouts)

2 Now translate the story.

Stage 3

3.1 Adjectives

In each sentence, (1) circle the adjective in parentheses that matches the picture, and (2) write an English translation of the completed sentence.

1 pāvō est (parātus / fortis).

_____

2 coquus est (īrātus / laetus).

_____

3 canis est (perterritus / īrātus).

_____

4 servus est (contentus / perterritus).

_____

3.2 How did Hercules kill the lion?

In Greek myth, killing the lion was the first of Hercules' twelve labors. This beast lived, near the Greek town of Nemea, in a tunnel-like cave open at both ends. Hercules had to block one end of the cave to keep the lion from escaping his reach.

Read the story below, and then write the answers to the questions at the bottom of the page.

Herculēs et leō

Herculēs magnum leōnem audit. leō ē cavernā venit. Herculēs nōn est perterritus. leō salit et Herculem petit. hērōs est fortis.
  "pestis!" inquit Herculēs.
  hērōs sagittam conicit. sagitta leōnem pulsat, sed mōnstrum nōn secat.
  "ēheu!" inquit Herculēs.
  hērōs fūstem tenet et leōnem verberat. leō rīdet; leō quoque est fortis.
  Herculēs est īrātus. "pestis! furcifer!" clāmat et leōnem strangulat.

Words and Phrases

ē cavernā	out of the cave
hērōs	hero
conicit	shoots
mōnstrum	monster
sagittam	arrow (Who is "Sagittarius"?)
strangulat	strangles

Questions

1 What are the insults Hercules shouts at the lion? _____
2 Which weapon does Hercules use first? _____
3 Which one second? _____
4 How, finally, does Hercules kill the lion? _____

5

Continued

More about Hercules

Do you know what happened to the lion after Hercules killed it?

Storytellers disagree about the fate of the Nemean lion. Some say that Hercules skinned it and, like some kind of caveman, wore the pelt around his shoulders with his head in the beast's scalp and his own eyes peering out through the open jaws. Others say that the lion became the constellation Leo.

Here are the Latin names of other constellations that are said to have been creatures killed by Hercules. Can you describe or draw them? (Use a separate sheet of paper.)

1 Aquila   2 Cancer   3 Centaurus   4 Draco   5 Hydra

3.3 What is the name?

Find the name of the region where Pompeii was located: first fill each set of blanks with a Latin adjective which translates the English. Then write the numbered letters in the order of their numbers in the space below.

```
                      5
angry         — — — — — —
              1
satisfied     — — — — — — — — —
                          2
busy          — — — — — — — — —
              4
terrified     — — — — — — — — — — —
              3
much          — — — — — —
                      7
very good     — — — — — — —
              8
happy         — — — — — —
                      6
big           — — — — — —
```

          1 2 3 4 5 6 7 8

Name: — — — — — — — —

3.4 What kind of person is he or she?

1 quālis coquus est Grumiō?
What kind of cook is Grumio?

Circle adjectives that describe
Grumio:

laetus

magnus

occupātus

multus

Graecus

2 quālis ancilla est Melissa?
What kind of slave-girl is Melissa?

Circle adjectives that describe
Melissa:

pulchra

occupāta

docta

magna

Graeca

3.5 How are these meanings related?

Write the number of each English word in front of the Latin word to which it
is related. Then, on a separate sheet of paper, explain how the meanings of
the English and the Latin word in each pair are related.

ENGLISH	LATIN
1 dominion	____ rīdet
2 dormitory	____ vīsitat
3 essential	____ portat
4 vinegar	____ canis
5 ridiculous	____ est
6 claim	____ dominus
7 village	____ vīnum
8 maternal	____ vīlla
9 kennel	____ māter
10 bib	____ dormit
11 porter	____ bibit
12 visit	____ clāmat

3.6 Roman Amphoras

Roman amphoras were usually large, plain earthenware jars with two handles (or "ears"), one on each side of a long neck. They were usually tall, with a sharp solid "toe" at the bottom so that they could be jammed upright in the ground or in a wooden rack.

By A.D. 79, the time of the stories in Unit 1, glass amphoras were also being used, but they were few when compared to the many earthenware jars discovered at Pompeii. (The process of blowing glass to make large, inexpensive jars had been discovered only some 100 years before.) The Romans used amphoras for storage and as transport containers for wine, olive oil, honey (they had no cane sugar in those days), a fish sauce called "garum," fruits like grapes and olives, and grain.

When the amphoras were filled, they were corked or stopped with plugs made of plaster, clay, or wood. Commercial amphoras intended for export, especially of wine, often had control "stamps" pressed (at the time of molding) into their handles. Stamped in the clay was the abbreviation of the exporter's name. This person backed with his name the true measure of the jars he had manufactured. Commercial amphoras were sometimes reused as coffins for babies or, laid end to end (with holes broken in), as makeshift drainage pipes.

Continued

Amphoras and their Modern Counterparts

On a separate sheet of paper, write the answers to the following:

1 In what types of stores and shops in Pompeii do you think archaeologists uncovered amphoras? If you can, find photographs of these stores in a good picture book of Pompeii.

2 Which modern goods are stored in paper or cloth sacks? Which in glass or plastic containers? (All these kinds of container are the contemporary versions of ancient amphoras.)

3 How is the capacity of modern glass or plastic containers marked? Where on the container?

Progress Check

Stages 1–3

20 items × 5 points = 100 points.

1 Choose from the lists below the correct name of the person shown in each picture. Write the name below the picture.

Caecilius	Grumiō	Metella	Syphāx
Celer	Herculēs	Pantagathus	
Cerberus	mercātor	Quīntus	

1 _____   2 _____

Continued

3 _____

4 _____

5 _____

6 _____

7 _____

8 _____

Continued

9 _____   10 _____

2 Fill the blank in each sentence with the correct word from the lists below.

amīcus   canis
ancilla   hērōs
argentārius   māter
fīlius   pictor
vēnālīcius   tōnsor

1 Pantagathus est _____ .

2 Syphāx est _____ .

3 Caecilius est _____ .

4 mercātor est _____ .

5 Metella est _____ .

6 Celer est _____ .

7 Melissa est _____ .

8 Cerberus est _____ .

9 Herculēs est _____ .

10 Quīntus est _____ .

Stage 4

4.1 How is Latin pronounced?

Perhaps Metella is pleased by Grumio's excellent pronunciation of Latin!

Metella Grumiōnem laudat.

Circle the English word that has the same (or almost the same) sound as the **boldfaced** letter in the Latin word.

1 f**ī**lius

city
ice
mater**i**al
leg**i**ble

2 in ātri**ō**

m**oo**n
t**oe**
b**oo**k
m**o**dern

3 p**a**ter

m**a**ke
s**a**d
f**a**r
alike

4 s**e**rvus

l**e**t
z**e**bra
b**e**tween
n**ee**dle

5 in c**u**līnā

under
f**u**me
f**u**ll
b**oo**t

6 Cae**c**ilius

simple
church
corner
spe**c**ial

7 Mete**ll**a

bri**ll**iant
papa**l** **l**egate
ha**ll**
lu**ll**aby

8 sur**g**it

Vir**g**inia
ga**g**
sovere**ig**n
sli**ng**

9 implu**v**ium

violin
wonder
bird
use

10 cibu**s**

pista**ch**io
refu**s**e
expre**ss**ion
simple

11 e**x**it

xylophone
o**x**
bi**g** **s**tep
xenon

12 Clēmē**n**s

a**n**swer
e**n**zyme
i**n**fants
i**n**surance

4.2 He or she?

1 First read each pair of Latin sentences. Then circle the correct pronoun in the English translation of the Latin verb in **boldface**.

    1 Caecilius Melissam spectat. ancillam **emit**.
      (He / She) buys . . .

    2 tōnsor tabernam habet. intentē **labōrat**.
      (He / She) works . . .

    3 Metella in viā ambulat. ad vīllam **revenit**.
      (He / She) is returning . . .

    4 poēta nāvem Syriam videt. Syphācem **vocat.**
      (He / She) calls . . .

    5 Clēmēns circumspectat. Cerberum **quaerit**.
      (He / She) is looking for . . .

    6 Melissa prope culīnam stat. Grumiōnem **exspectat**.
      (He / She) is waiting for . . .

2 Write a complete translation for each of the six pairs of Latin sentences.

4.3 What are you doing?

Circle the correct verb-form when a choice is provided in brackets. If you cannot remember the correct ending, consult p. 204 of your textbook.

1 Caecilius says, "Celer is painting."
Caecilius asks,
  "quid tū (pingō / pingis)?"

Celer answers,
  "ego leōnem (pingō / pingis)."

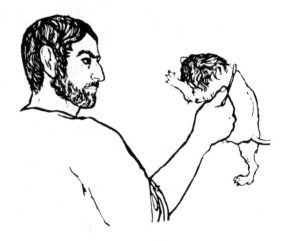

2 Metella says, "Clemens is carrying something."
Metella asks,
  "quid tū (portās / portō)?"
Clemens answers,
  "ego vīnum (portās / portō)."

3 Caecilius says, "The old man sees something."
Caecilius asks,
  "quid tū (vidēs / videō)?"
The old man answers,
  "ego novāculam (vidēs / videō)."

4 The poet says, "Hermogenes has something."
The poet asks,
  "quid tū (habeō / habēs)?"
Hermogenes answers,
  "ego pecūniam (habeō / habēs)."

5 Quintus says, "Syphax is selling someone."
Quintus asks,
  "quem tū (vēndō / vēndis)?"
Syphax answers,
  "ego Melissam (vēndō / vēndis)."

4.4 The Lares

As every Roman town had a temple of its "larēs", or guardian spirits, so an individual family had a "larārium," or small shrine, for the household lares.

The lares in the household shrine were often imagined as young men wearing tunics and many bronze statuettes of these have been found. They hold, in a raised hand, a "rhyton," and in a lowered hand, a "patera." A patera was a large saucer that the Romans used for drinking and for offering libations. A rhyton was a drinking horn with a hole at the bottom point from which a person drank wine. The statuettes of lares may remind us, by their pose, of modern ballet dancers.

Because the lares – as spirits that loved the family – guarded it well, they were easily associated with dogs. Sometimes a statuette of a dog was set beside them. At every meal, the family gave the lares a small portion of food. This was set in front of the statuettes in small dishes. On special occasions the family hung flower-wreaths around the lares' necks. Such occasions might have been the safe return of a father from a trip or after military service, the arrival of a new bride, or a young man's reaching the age of maturity.

About the Lararium

In Stages 1 (p.3) and 2 (pp. 20–21), the lararium of Caecilius' house is illustrated several times. First find and study the pictures. Then write the answers to the following:

1   In which room of Caecilius' house was the lararium located?

_____

2   Does the upper half of the lararium remind you of a Classical building?
_____ If yes, which kind?_____

Continued

Additional Projects

1 In the pictures of your textbook, the lares themselves are very small. On a sheet of poster paper, draw Caecilius' lararium very large and include the lares in their proper place. Don't forget the dog!

2 In illustrated books about Pompeii, look through the pictures of house-interiors and find as many different lararia as you can. What animal was often painted on the wall at the back of a lararium? Why do you think this animal was painted there? Write your answer below.

4.5 Find the verbs

In the box of letters below, you will find fourteen verbs with the ending **-T** (e.g. INQUI**T**). Find each verb and circle it.

```
I N Q U I T T U A G I T P E R T E R R I T U S F O R U M
E T R E D D I T Q U A E R I T P O E T A T U M U L T U S
H A B E T M E T E L L A M V E N D I T S A T I S Q U I D
C U R V O C A T C E R A M C O Q U I T E X S P E C T A T
V I L L A M T A B E R N A C I R C U M S P E C T A T I N
M E R C A T O R A M I C U S V I N U M N O N G U S T A T
T U C I B U M E T E C C E B I B I T R I D E T I A N U A
P I C T O R T O N S O R E M S U R G I T F O R T I S E T
```

Stage 5

5.1 One or many?

First study each picture and then circle the sentence that correctly describes it.

1   mercātōrēs hodiē sunt occupātī.
mercātor hodiē est occupātus.

2   nāvēs in portū stant.
nāvis in portū stat.

3   Pompēiānī in forō ambulant.
Pompēiānus in forō ambulat.

5.2 Where is the gold?

The Roman playwright Plautus, in the 2nd century B.C., wrote a hilarious play called *Aulularia*, or "Pot of Gold." The action of this comedy centers around a miser named Euclio. (He hides his gold coins in a common kitchen pot, or "aulula.")

Because misers are penny-pinchers, you may imagine them as people without feelings. But a miser is a man in love. Although he doesn't love a woman, his work, or even himself, he is nevertheless madly in love with his money.

The following playlet is based on an episode in the *Aulularia*.

Eucliō et aulula

Euclio comes home from the forum hiding a pot under his tunic.

Eucliō (senex):	ego sum pauper. ego pecūniam nōn habeō. ego cibum nōn emō.
amīcus:	tū es pauper? ecce! tū vīllam et servum habēs. tū aululam tenēs.
Eucliō:	ego aululam teneō? ēheu! amīcus aurum meum videt. 5 (*Eucliō exit et aululam in culīnā cēlat. Eucliō revenit.*) ecce! ego aululam nōn teneō. ego nunc sum pauper.

Congriō subitō intrat. Congriō aululam tenet.

Congriō (coquus):	ego in culīnā dormiō. ecce! ego iānuam audiō. ego surgō et multum aurum in aululā inveniō. euge! ego 10 nunc sum dominus.
Eucliō:	tū es dominus? (*senex aululam rapit.*) Eucliō est dominus, et tū nōn es Eucliō. tū es furcifer! (*coquus in culīnam currit.*)

Words and Phrases

aulula	pot
pauper	poor
aurum	gold
ego inveniō	I find
nunc	now
rapit	grabs

Continued

About the Playlet

Although the playlet above is short, you can easily imagine the look and personality of the characters. They are simple, and some of the characters in your Unit 1 textbook are very similar. Euclio is like Lucrio in Stage 5, and Congrio is like Grumio in Stage 2.

Write the answers to the following:

1   What kind of person is Congrio or Grumio?

_____

_____

2   What kind of person is Euclio or Lucrio?

_____

_____

5.3 Who is in the picture?

Beneath each picture, write the Latin noun that identifies the character or characters in it. Choose the correct noun from the lists below (there are more than you will need).

canis	puer	canēs	puerī
poēta	servus	poētae	servī
puella	vēnālīcius	puellae	vēnālīciī

(singular nominative noun)   *(plural nominative noun)*

1 _____   **2** _____

24   Continued

3 _____

4 _____

5 _____

6 _____

7 _____

8 _____

5.4 Which is correct?

1 Which word describes more than one person?

Circle the plural noun:

Clēmēns

Poppaea

Pompēiānī

Melissa

Caecilius

2 Which word describes only one person?

Circle the singular noun:

fēminae

mercātōrēs

iuvenis

puerī

pāstōrēs

3 Which word describes staying in one place?

ambulat

contendit

ruit

currit

manet

4 Which sentence describes an action of Cerberus?

. . . . . ānulum cēlat.

. . . . . cibum emit.

. . . . . in viā dormit.

. . . . . pecūniam dēbet.

. . . . . argentāriam habet.

5 Which sentence describes someone having a good time?

. . . . . negōtium agit.

. . . . . signum imprimit.

. . . . . barbam tondet.

. . . . . fūnambulum spectat.

. . . . . basilicam intrat.

6 Which sentence describes an action of Caecilius?

. . . . . Melissam vēndit.

. . . . . fābulam agit.

. . . . . cēnam coquit.

. . . . . Melissam emit.

. . . . . in mēnsā stat.

Stage 6

6.1 What is happening?

First study each picture and then circle the verb in parentheses which correctly describes what is happening.

1 Caecilius pecūniam (numerābat / scrībēbat).

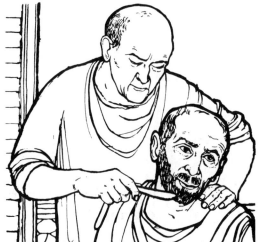

2 Pantagathus barbam (bibēbat / tondēbat).

3 Caecilius in forō (iacēbat / stābat).

Continued

4 poēta versum Graecum (recitābat / pulsābat).

5 Pompēiānī negōtium in forō (pingēbant / agēbant).

6 coquus pāvōnem (parāvit / verberāvit).

7 fēminae iuvenem (dēlectāvērunt / necāvērunt).

6.2 postquam- and quod-Clauses

Fill the blanks in each English sentence with a translation of the Latin verb in boldface. Include the correct pronoun: "he," "she," "they," or "I."

1 Grumiō, postquam leōnem in pictūrā **vituperāvit**, ē triclīniō festīnāvit.

   Grumio, after _____ _____ the lion in the picture, hurried out of the dining-room.

2 Caecilius, quod **erat** īrātus, Hermogenem ad basilicam vocāvit.

   Caecilius, because _____ _____ angry, summoned Hermogenes to the law court.

3 Caecilius, postquam Hermogenem **accūsāvit**, tōtam rem nārrāvit.

   Caecilius, after _____ _____ Hermogenes, told the whole story.

4 ego serpentem in cubiculō habeō, quod **sum** senex et sōlus.

   I have a snake in my bedroom, because _____ _____ an old man and alone.

5 Grumiō aberat, quod Poppaeam **vīsitābat**.

   Grumio was absent, because _____ _____ _____ Poppaea.

6 Lucriō aberat, quod ad theātrum **contendēbat**.

   Lucrio was absent, because _____ _____ _____ to the theater.

7 Fēlīx nihil audīvit, quod in tablīnō **scrībēbat.**

   Felix heard nothing, because _____ _____ _____ in the study.

8 fūrēs, postquam serpentem intentē **spectāvērunt**, ē cubiculō festīnāvērunt.

   The thieves, after _____ _____ intently at the snake, hurried out of the bedroom.

6.3 What is the Latin message?

First fill each set of blanks with the letters of an English word which is related to the Latin one in brackets. Use the English definition to help you find the English word that fits the blanks.

Then write the numbered letters in the order of their numbers in the spaces provided.

First word of message:

(currit)	flow, as of electricity	__ __ __ __ __ __ __ *(4 over 7th blank)*
(cubiculum)	small space or compartment	__ __ __ __ __ __ __ *(2 over 2nd blank)*
(dormit)	inactive	__ __ __ __ __ __ __ *(6 over 3rd blank)*
(ambulat)	vehicle for carrying sick	__ __ __ __ __ __ __ __ __ *(1 over 2nd blank)*
(fābula)	story with a moral	__ __ __ __ __ *(3 over 4th blank)*
(coquit)	bread in small, rough cake	__ __ __ __ __ __ __ *(5 over 5th blank)*

1 2 3 4 5 6

Hidden Latin word (1): __ __ __ __ __ __

Second word of message:

(scrībit)	sacred book	__ __ __ __ __ __ __ __ __ *(4 over 2nd blank)*
(fortis)	a large fort	__ __ __ __ __ __ __ *(6 over 6th blank)*
(clāmat)	assert as a fact	__ __ __ __ __ *(2 over 4th blank)*
(signum)	make known by signs	__ __ __ __ __ __ *(5 over 1st blank)*
(vēndit)	person who sells things	__ __ __ __ __ __ *(1 over 5th blank)*
(manet)	large or stately residence	__ __ __ __ __ __ __ *(3 over 4th blank)*

1 2 3 4 5 6

Hidden Latin word (2): __ __ __ __ __ __

Read and translate the hidden message:

30

6.4 Which is the correct English pronoun?

Fill each blank with the correct English pronoun: "He," "She," or "They."
The pronoun should match in meaning the **boldfaced** Latin word or words
in the first of each set of sentences.

1 **pāstōrēs** are coming down from the mountain today.

_____ are going to the theater to watch a play.

2 **Actius et Sorex** are here.

_____ are going to the theater to perform.

3 **puella** watches the actors.

_____ applauds them.

4 Where are **fēminae et** other **puellae**?

_____ are already sitting in the theater.

5 **iuvenis** looks at the girl.

_____ is pleased.

6 **senex** looks at the crowd.

_____ is frightened.

7 **Grumiō** is not cooking dinner today.

_____ is out of the house.

8 Why isn't **Poppaea** sitting in the theater?

_____ is at home waiting for Grumio.

9 **ancilla** sees Caecilius.

"Hello!"_____ says.

10 "Hello!" says **dominus.**

_____ is going to the theater too.

Progress Check

Stages 4–6

10 items × 10 points = 100 points

1 Circle the correct noun- or verb-form in each sentence.

1 (māter / mātrem) fūrem pulsābat.

2 fūr (mātrem / māter) superāvit.

3 (īnfāns / īnfantem) fūrem spectābat.

4 fūr (īnfāns / īnfantem) petīvit.

5 servī fūrem (verberābat / verberābant).

6 pater fūrem (necāvērunt / necāvit).

2 Circle the correct verb-form in each pair of brackets.

1 tū amīcum ad vīllam (invītās / invītat);

ego (sum / es) sōlus.

2 tū cēnam optimam (parat / parās);

ego nihil (cōnsūmit / cōnsūmō).

3 amīcus vīllam (intrat / intrās);
ego in viā (manēs / maneō).

4 tū (es / est) laetus;

ego (lacrimō / lacrimat).

3 For 1 extra point of credit each:
On a separate sheet of paper, write a translation for each of the sentences in paragraphs 1 and 2 above.

Stage 7

7.1 Who did it?

First look at the character or characters in each picture and read the Latin sentence beside it.

Then write an English translation beneath the Latin sentence using the correct English pronoun: "He," "She," or "They."

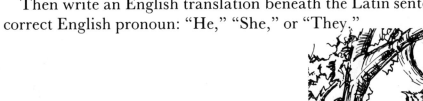

1   subitō appāruit.

_____

2   āctōrem spectāvērunt.

_____

3   cibum gustāvit.

_____

Continued

4 canem cōnspexit.

_____

5 vīnum laudāvit.

_____

6 Quīntum salūtāvit.

_____

7 per viam prōcessērunt.

_____

7.2 Today or yesterday?

In each Latin sentence, circle the verb-form in parentheses which correctly translates the **boldfaced** English word or words.

1 Grumio **is cooking** the peacock.
   Grumiō pāvōnem (coxit / coquit).

2 The centurion **had** a tunic.
   centuriō tunicam (habet / habuit).

3 My friend **understood** the truth.
   amīcus rem (intellēxit / intellegit).

4 Melissa **praised** the actor.
   Melissa āctōrem (laudat / laudāvit).

5 The slave **is departing** from the city.
   servus ex urbe (discessit / discēdit).

6 The dogs **frightened** the boy.
   canēs puerum (terruērunt / terrent).

7 The hunters **heard** the racket.
   vēnātōrēs clāmōrem (audīvērunt / audiunt).

8 The slaves **caught sight** of Decens.
   servī Decentem (cōnspiciunt / cōnspexērunt).

9 Grumio and Clemens **found fault with** Melissa.
   Grumiō et Clēmēns Melissam (vituperant / vituperāvērunt).

10 Werewolves **do** not **appear** often!
   versipellēs nōn saepe (appāruērunt / appārent)!

11 The actor **advanced** towards the stage.
   āctor ad scaenam (prōcēdit / prōcessit).

12 The poet **is walking** in the garden.
   poēta in hortō (ambulat / ambulāvit).

7.3 What do you see in the picture?

First study the picture and then circle the names of all the objects and persons that are pictured, either whole or in part.

amīcus
Caecilius
cibus
cubiculum
hortus
lectus

leō
lupus
mēnsa
pōculum
Quīntus
triclīnium

7.4 Find the verbs

In the box of letters below, you will find fifteen verbs with the ending **-nt** (e.g. **ABSUNT**). The tense will be present, imperfect, or perfect. Find each verb and circle it.

```
A B S U N T A G I T A G U N T E M I S E R U N T
B I B I T E T T U T A N D E M B I B U N T T U M
C U R R E B A N T B I B E R U N T E S T T U U S
N O N T A C I T E D O R M I V E R U N T E X I T
E X S P E C T A N T T E R R E B A N T T A M E N
T E R R E N T E T P R O C E S S E R U N T E S T
P L A U S I T C O N T E N D E R U N T T U R B A
C O N T E N D E B A N T E S T T U M V O C A N T
E X N O N T U R B A V E N E R U N T T E R R A M
```

7.5 What were Roman ghosts said to eat?

Find the English names of two different foods which were left beside tombs as food for the ghosts of the dead.

First fill each set of blanks with a Latin word which translates the English. Then write the numbered letters in the order of their numbers in the spaces provided.

First food offering:

all	$\underset{}{\_} \ \underset{}{\_} \ \underset{}{\_} \ \underset{4}{\_} \ \underset{}{\_}$
ghost	$\underset{}{\_} \ \underset{}{\_} \ \underset{1}{\_} \ \underset{}{\_} \ \underset{}{\_}$
hits	$\underset{}{\_} \ \underset{}{\_} \ \underset{}{\_} \ \underset{5}{\_} \ \underset{}{\_} \ \underset{}{\_}$
understands	$\underset{}{\_} \ \underset{}{\_} \ \underset{}{\_} \ \underset{2}{\_} \ \underset{}{\_} \ \underset{}{\_} \ \underset{}{\_} \ \underset{}{\_} \ \underset{}{\_} \ \underset{}{\_}$
asks	$\underset{}{\_} \ \underset{}{\_} \ \underset{}{\_} \ \underset{3}{\_} \ \underset{}{\_}$

1   2   3   4   5

Food (1): _ _ _ _ _

Second food offering:

announces	$\underset{}{\_} \ \underset{}{\_} \ \underset{3}{\_} \ \underset{}{\_} \ \underset{}{\_} \ \underset{}{\_} \ \underset{}{\_}$
walks	$\underset{}{\_} \ \underset{}{\_} \ \underset{}{\_} \ \underset{}{\_} \ \underset{6}{\_} \ \underset{}{\_} \ \underset{}{\_}$
wine cup	$\underset{}{\_} \ \underset{}{\_} \ \underset{}{\_} \ \underset{1}{\_} \ \underset{}{\_} \ \underset{}{\_} \ \underset{}{\_}$
thing	$\underset{}{\_} \ \underset{}{\_} \ \underset{7}{\_}$
suddenly	$\underset{}{\_} \ \underset{}{\_} \ \underset{}{\_} \ \underset{4}{\_} \ \underset{}{\_} \ \underset{}{\_}$
beautiful	$\underset{}{\_} \ \underset{}{\_} \ \underset{}{\_} \ \underset{}{\_} \ \underset{2}{\_} \ \underset{}{\_} \ \underset{}{\_}$
freedman	$\underset{}{\_} \ \underset{5}{\_} \ \underset{}{\_} \ \underset{}{\_} \ \underset{}{\_} \ \underset{}{\_} \ \underset{}{\_} \ \underset{}{\_}$

1   2   3   4   5   6   7

Food (2): _ _ _ _ _ _ _

Stage 8

8.1 How did rich Romans entertain?

Seneca the Younger was a writer contemporary with Petronius, the writer who recorded the original version of the "fābula mīrābilis" in Stage 7. Because both writers were officials in the court of the Emperor Nero (who ruled A.D. 54–68), they may have known each other well.

The following anecdote about a rich Roman's dinner party is based on an account in a letter written by Seneca.

Calvisius et servī

Calvisius poētās Graecōs et antīquōs amābat. hic dominus pecūniam multam habēbat et quattuor servōs doctōs ā vēnālīciō ēmit. saepe multī amīcī cum Calvisiō cēnābant. omnēs coquum laudābant, quod cēna erat optima; Calvisium laudābant, quod erat hospes optimus.

ōlim, postquam amīcī in lectīs recubuērunt, servī poētās Graecōs 5
commendāvērunt. prīmus servus Homērum commendāvit; secundus
Hēsiodum; tertius Sapphōnem; quārtus Alcaeum. postquam servī poētās
Graecōs commendāvērunt, omnēs amīcī plausērunt.

"Calvisī," inquit amīcus, "Graecōs librōs habēs?"

"ego librōs nōn habeō," respondit Calvisius. "sed servōs doctissimōs 10
habeō."

Words and Phrases

antīquōs	ancient
quattuor	four
commendāvērunt	recommended
Homērum	Homer; Greek epic poet in 8th century B.C.
Hēsiodum	Hesiod; Greek epic poet in 8th century B.C.
tertius	third
Sapphōnem	Sappho: Greek lyric woman poet in 6th century B.C.
quārtus	fourth
Alcaeum	Alcaeus; Greek lyric poet in 6th century B.C.

Questions

On a separate sheet of paper, write the answers to the following:

1 How do you think the slaves had gotten to know about Greek literature?
2 Why do you think Calvisius liked to have slaves who could recommend Greek authors, although he did not have Greek books?

8.2 Which is the correct accusative?

First study each picture and then circle the noun-form in parentheses which correctly describes it.

1 amīcus (canem / canēs) cōnspexit.

2 Caecilius (cīvem Pompēiānum / cīvēs Pompēiānōs) spectabat.

3 Caecilius (canem / canēs) cōnspexit.

Continued

4 Pompēiānī (nūntiōs / nūntium) audiēbant.

5 spectātōrēs (murmillōnem / murmillōnēs) incitābant.

6 bēstiāriī (bēstiās / bēstiam) necābant.

7 bēstiārius (leōnem / leōnēs) necāvit.

8.3 Superlatives

In each Latin sentence, circle the adjective or adverb in parentheses which correctly translates the **boldface** English word or words.

1 The spectators were **very happy** then.

tum spectātōrēs erant (laetī / laetissimī).

2 The gladiators were **brave**.

gladiātōrēs erant (fortēs / fortissimī).

3 The net-fighter killed the murmillo **as quickly as possible**.

rētiārius murmillōnem (quam celerrimē / celeriter) interfēcit.

4 The wolves killed the dogs **quickly**.

lupī canēs (celerrimē / celeriter) interfēcērunt.

5 You are holding back the **most ferocious** boars.

tū aprōs (ferōcēs / ferōcissimōs) retinēs.

6 Gaius liked the **very big** picture.

Gāius pictūram (maximam / magnam) amābat.

7 The picture was expensive, because it was **very beautiful.**

pictūra erat pretiōsa, quod erat (pulchra / pulcherrima).

8 Your dress is **beautiful**.

stola tua est (pulcherrima / pulchra).

9 My dog is **big**.

canis meus est (magnus / maximus).

10 The dogs killed the deer **very quickly**.

canēs cervōs (celeriter / celerrimē) interfēcērunt.

11 Yesterday the ghost was **very angry**.

heri umbra erat (īrātissima / īrāta).

12 Today the ghost is **satisfied**.

hodiē umbra est (contentissima / contenta).

8.4 After what did it happen?

In the two examples following, compare the order of the words in **boldface**:

Latin: **Pompēiānī, postquam** nūntiōs audīvērunt, ad amphitheātrum contendērunt.

English: **After the Pompeians** heard the messengers, they hurried to the amphitheater.

Now fill the blanks in each English sentence with the best translation of the Latin words in **boldface**.

1   **Rēgulus, postquam** hunc clāmōrem audīvit, leōnēs nōn retinuit.

_____ _____ heard this noise, he did not hold back the lions.

2   **leō, postquam** fremuit, pedem ostendit.

_____ _____ _____ roared, he showed his paw.

3   **pāstor, postquam** ad leōnem cautē vēnit, pedem īnspexit.

_____ _____ _____ came cautiously toward the lion, he inspected the paw.

4   **Androclēs, postquam** leōnem cūrāvit, ad urbem festīnāvit.

_____ _____ took care of the lion, he hurried to the city.

5   **leō, postquam** Androclem agnōvit, lambēbat.

_____ _____ _____ recognized Androcles, he licked him.

Stage 9

9.1 To whom?

First study each picture and then circle the noun in parentheses that correctly describes what is happening.

Finally, write an English translation beneath each Latin sentence.

1 Caecilius (Metellae / Syphācī) pecūniam dedit.

_____

2 mercātor (gladiātōrī / Metellae) pōculum ostendit.

_____

_____

3 Quīntus (amīcīs / lupīs) fābulam splendidam nārrāvit.

_____

_____

9.2 Who was the original Milo?

Milo the discus-thrower of Stage 9—the nose of whose statue was broken by Quintus—is an imaginary athlete, though typical of his time. He was appropriately named, however, since the Greeks and Romans had long told stories about a legendary sports "star" also named Milo.

The original Milo came from the Greek colony of Croton, on the "instep" of Italy. If this Milo was ever a real person, he would have lived in the 6th century B.C.

This is an account of the best-known episode in the first Milo's long athletic career, and also of his unusually violent death.

luctātor Milō

Milō erat Graecus āthlēta. Milō erat luctātor fortissimus. sexiēs in Olympicīs lūdīs, sexiēs in Pȳthiīs lūdīs erat victor. Milō erat nōtissimus, et omnēs Graecī hērōem laudāvērunt.

hic āthlēta saepe in palaestrā sē exercēbat, et cīvēs fābulam mīrābilem nārrābant: "ōlim Milō taurum dē monte portāvit. hērōs, postquam hunc taurum ūnō ictū necāvit, tōtum taurum cōnsūmpsit." Milō ingentissimus ē palaestrā prōcēdēbat. spectātōrēs, postquam Milōnem vīdērunt, domum contendēbant. fābulam dē taurō fēminīs et servīs nārrābant. 5

posteā Milō iterum ad montem prōcessit. ēheu! lupī ferōcissimī Milōnem vīvum cōnsūmpsērunt. 10

Words and Phrases

luctātor	wrestler
sexiēs	six times
in Olympicīs lūdīs	in the Olympic games; celebrated at Olympia, Greece
in Pȳthiīs lūdīs	in the Pythian games; celebrated at Delphi, Greece
taurum	bull
ūnō ictū	with one blow (of the hand)
tōtum	whole
domum	home
vīvum	alive

Questions

On a separate sheet of paper, write the answers to the following:

1 Do you know any stories about sports stars that are hard to believe, but nevertheless true? If so, write out one of them.
2 Do wrestlers still have the high status in the sports world that they once had in ancient Greece? Why?

9.3 For whom?

First study each picture and then circle the noun in parentheses that correctly describes the scene.

Finally, write an English translation beneath each Latin sentence.

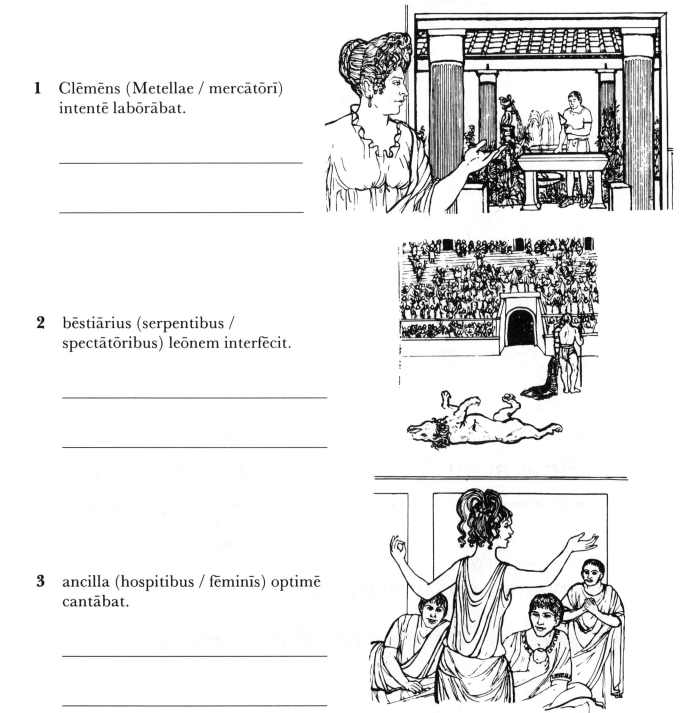

1 Clēmēns (Metellae / mercātōrī) intentē labōrābat.

_____

_____

2 bēstiārius (serpentibus / spectātōribus) leōnem interfēcit.

_____

_____

3 ancilla (hospitibus / fēminīs) optimē cantābat.

_____

_____

9.4 bēstiārius et bēstiae

Make each sentence describe the picture by circling the correct Latin words;
then translate it.

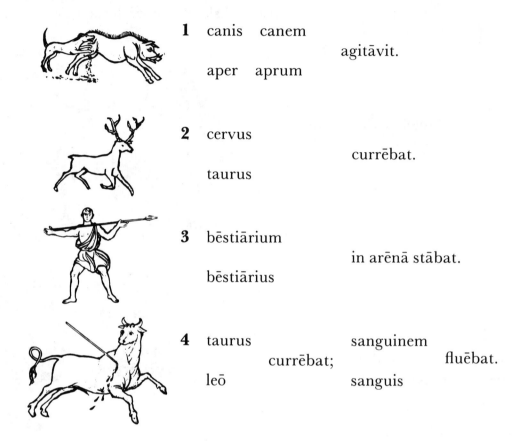

1 canis   canem

                     agitāvit.

  aper   aprum

2 cervus

                  currēbat.

  taurus

3 bēstiārium

                 in arēnā stābat.

  bēstiārius

4 taurus   sanguinem

           currēbat;   fluēbat.

  leō   sanguis

9.5 How many Latin words can you find?

Put together as many Latin words as you can, using only the letters in the
following sentence:

CIVES NUNTIOS AUDIVERUNT.

List your words on a separate sheet of paper.
Some examples are VISITAT, OSTENDIT, and DISCUS.

Progress Check

Stages 7–9

25 items × 4 points = 100 points

1 Write the number of each word in column A in front of its English or Latin translation in column B.

	A		B
1	asks	____	brings
2	blood	____	cōnspicit
3	catches sight of	____	diēs
4	day	____	hands over
5	fert	____	rogat
6	incitat	____	sanguis
7	trādit	____	trumpet
8	tuba	____	urges on

2 Fill the blank in each chart below with the missing Latin noun-form. (sg. = singular; pl. = plural)

1 porta	_____ (nominative pl.)	2 lībertus	lībertī
portam	portās	lībertum	_____ (accusative pl.)
3 _____ (nominative sg.)	umbrae	4 centuriō	centuriōnēs
umbram	umbrās	_____ (accusative sg.)	centuriōnēs
5 nūntius	nūntiī	6 āctor	_____ (nominative pl.)
_____ (accusative sg.)	nūntiōs	āctōrem	āctōrēs
7 puer	_____ (nominative pl.)	8 homō	hominēs
puerum	puerōs	hominem	_____ (accusative pl.)

Continued

3 Fill the blank in each set below with the missing Latin verb-form.

1 _____ intellēxērunt
  (s/he) understood   (they) understood

2 lacrimāvit
  (s/he) wept   _____
                      (they) wept

3 _____ necāvērunt
  (s/he) killed   (they) killed

4 parāvit   _____
  (s/he) prepared   (they) prepared

5 prōcessit   _____
  (s/he) advanced   (they) advanced

6 terruit   _____
  (s/he) frightened   (they) frightened

7 _____ habuērunt
  (s/he) had   (they) had

8 agnōvit   _____
  (s/he) recognized   (they) recognized

9 _____ audīvērunt
  (s/he) heard   (they) heard

Stage 10

10.1 Which is the correct verb?

In each Latin sentence, circle the verb-form in parentheses which is correct.
If you cannot remember the correct ending, consult pp. 204–205 of your
textbook.

1   ego (sum / sumus) coquus.
    ego cēnam (parāmus / parō).

2   ego (sumus / sum) ancilla.
    ego suāviter (cantō / cantāmus).

3   tū (estis / es) mercātor.
    tū mihi togam (ostendis / ostenditis).

4   tū (es / estis) gladiātor.
    tū missiōnem (postulātis / postulās).

5   vōs Nūcerīnī (es / estis) turbulentī.
    vōs amphitheātrum et omnēs viās (complēs / complētis).

6   nōs Pompēiānī (sumus / sum) īrātī.
    nōs gladiōs (vibrō / vibrāmus).

10.2 Which adjective fits the person?

Match the name of the person or persons in column 1 with the adjective in column 2 which correctly describes him, her, or them. Draw a line between them.

1	2
Decēns	docta
Herculēs	expedītī
īnfāns	fortis
Melissa	mortuus
rētiāriī	parvus

10.3 Which is the correct form?

1 Match the adjective in column 1 with its comparative form in column 2. Draw a line between them.

1	2	
pulcher	maior	_____
magnus	pulchrior	_____
ingēns	nōtior	_____
nōtus	ingentior	_____

2 Write an English translation for each of the comparative forms in column 2.

3 Match the adjective in column 1 with its superlative form in column 2. Draw a line between them.

1	2	
ignāvus	fortissimus	_____
inimīcus	ferōcissimus	_____
fortis	inimīcissimus	_____
ferōx	ignāvissimus	_____

4 Write an English translation for each of the superlative forms in column 2.

10.4 Narcissus

Just up from Caecilius' house on Stabiae Street, in a house now called the House of the *Ara Maxima* "Very Large Altar," an unknown painter painted on the wall a picture of the tragic young man Narcissus.

This is a retelling of the story in Latin.

Narcissus

pictor iuvenem Graecum pingit. hic iuvenis est Narcissus. Narcissus est pulcherrimus. prope aquam sedet et sē in aquā spectat.

ōlim Narcissus erat vēnātor. vēnābulum longum capiēbat et multī amīcī cum eō ad vēnātiōnem ībant. Narcissus tamen nōn leōnēs ferōcēs in monte petēbat, sed cervōs perterritōs in silvā obscūrā inveniēbat et trānsfīgēbat.   5
Narcissus erat vēnātor ignāvissimus.

nunc Narcissus sedet sōlus. aquam nōn bibit, sed imāginem suam semper spectat. imāginem amat. iuvenis nōn est pulchrior quam imāgō sua.

"tū es pulcherrimus," Narcissus imāginī dīcit. "dēliciae meae! tē amō. tū mē amās?" sed imāgō Narcissō nihil dīcit.   10

cotīdiē rogat Narcissus, "tū mē amās?" cotīdiē nihil respondet imāgō. Narcissus stat, et imāgō stat. Narcissus sedet, et imāgō sedet. Narcissus lacrimat, et imāgō lacrimat. Narcissus clāmat, sed imāgō nōn clāmat.

nunc moribundus, "dēliciae meae! tū mē amās?" rogat Narcissus. imāgō Narcissum spectat. sed tacet. ēheu! Narcissus est mortuus.   15

Words and Phrases

cum eō	with him
aquam	water
imāginem	image, reflection

Questions

On a separate sheet of paper, write the answers to the following:

1 In what country did Narcissus supposedly live?
2 What kind of animals did Narcissus prefer to hunt? Was he a brave hunter?
3 Why did Narcissus look at his reflection in the pool of water?
4 Why do you think Narcissus eventually died?
5 What does the English word *narcissism* mean? What is the connection between this meaning and the story of Narcissus?

10.5 Make your own sentences

1 On a separate sheet of paper, write at least ten different Latin sentences from the words in the columns below.

To compose a Latin sentence, choose one word from column 1, one from 2, one from 3, etc. (There is no choice in columns 2 and 4.) Keep the words in the 1–2–3–4–5 order.

For example,

1	2	3	4	5	
puella	est	pulchrior	quam	puer.	The girl is more beautiful than the boy.

1	2	3	4	5
dominus	est	ferōcior	quam	dominus
fēmina		fortior		ego
frāter		ingentior		fēmina
hospes		maior		frāter
ille homō		nōtior		hospes
iuvenis		pulchrior		ille homō
puella				iuvenis
puer				puella
uxor				puer
				tū
				uxor

(*nominative singular noun*)		(*comparative nominative singular adjective*)		(*nominative singular pronoun or noun*)

2 Write a translation for each of your sentences.

10.6 Who is bigger? Who is smaller?

First study the picture on the next page and then mark it according to instructions.

1 Mark an 'x' under the picture of the *iuvenis* who is *maior*.

2 Mark a 'y' under the picture of the *puella* who is *minor*.

Continued

10.7 Make your own sentences

1 On a separate sheet of paper, write at least ten different Latin sentences from the words in the columns below.

To compose a Latin sentence, choose one word from column 1, one from 2, one from 3, etc. (There is no choice in columns 2 and 4.) Keep the words in the 1–2–3–4–5 order.

For example,

1	2	3	4	5	
āthlētae	sunt	nōtiōrēs	quam	coquī.	The athletes are more famous than the cooks.

1	2	3	4	5
ancillae	sunt	ferōciōrēs	quam	ancillae
āthlētae		fortiōrēs		āthlētae
caupōnēs		ingentiōrēs		caupōnēs
coquī		maiōrēs		coquī
gladiātōrēs		nōtiōrēs		gladiātōrēs
illī hominēs		pulchriōrēs		illī hominēs
pistōrēs				nōs
rhētorēs				pistōrēs
vēnālīciī				rhētorēs
				vēnālīciī
				vōs
(nominative plural noun		*(comparative nominative plural adjective)*		*(nominative plural pronoun or noun)*

2 Write a translation for each of your sentences.

Stage 11

11.1 Whom does he support?

magna turba est in forō, quod multī cīvēs candidātōs īnspiciunt.

Instructions: In each Latin sentence below, circle the noun-form in parentheses that correctly translates the **boldfaced** English words.

1a The farmer greets **the farmer.**

agricola (agricolam / agricolae) salūtat.

1b The farmer gives his support **to the farmer**.

agricola (agricolam / agricolae) favet.

2a The baker greets **the baker**.

pistor (pistōrī / pistōrem) salūtat.

2b The baker has faith **in the baker**.

pistor (pistōrī / pistōrem) crēdit.

3a The merchant greets **the merchant**.

mercātor (mercātōrī / mercātōrem) salūtat.

3b The merchant gives his support **to the merchant**

mercātor (mercātōrem / mercātōrī) favet.

Continued

4a The young man greets **his candidate**; the candidate is an athlete.

iuvenis (candidātō / candidātum) salūtat; candidātus est āthlēta.

4b The young man has faith **in the athlete**.

iuvenis (āthlētae / āthlētam) crēdit.

5a The thief greets **a very bad** candidate; the candidate is a thief too.

fūr candidātum (pessimum / pessimō) salūtat; candidātus quoque est fūr.

5b The thief has faith **in the thief**.

fūr (fūrem / fūrī) crēdit.

11.2 To whom?

Instructions: In the question-and-answer pairs below, circle in each answer the Latin noun-form in parentheses that translates the **boldfaced** English word or words.

1 Q "Are you Lucius Spurius Pomponianus?" Clemens asked.

"tūne es Lūcius Spurius Pompōniānus?" rogāvit Clēmēns.

A "Today I am a citizen of Pompeii," Grumio replied **to Clemens**.

"hodiē ego sum cīvis Pompēiānus," Grumiō (Clēmentem / Clēmentī) respondit.

Continued

2 Q "Surely you are not a citizen?" Clemens asked.

"num tū es cīvis?" rogāvit Clēmēns.

A "Today I am a citizen. I am a baker and I am supporting **Afer**," Grumio said **to Clemens**.

"hodiē ego sum cīvis. ego sum pistor et (Āfrum / Āfrō) faveō," Grumiō (Clēmentem / Clēmentī) dīxit.

3 Q "Why are you supporting Afer?"

"cūr tū Āfrō favēs?"

"All we bakers trust **Afer**," said Grumio.

"nōs pistōrēs omnēs (Āfrō / Āfrum) crēdimus," inquit Grumiō.

4 Q "Do you bakers trust **Holconius**?" Clemens asked Grumio.

"vōsne pistōrēs (Holcōnium / Holcōniō) crēditis?" Clēmēns Grumiōnem rogāvit.

A "We do not trust **Holconius**," Grumio replied **to Clemens**. "Holconius is **very bad**."

"nōs (Holcōniō / Holcōnium) nōn crēdimus," Grumiō (Clēmentī / Clēmentem) respondit. "Holcōnius est (optimus / pessimus)."

5 Q "Where is Afer now?"

"ubi nunc est Āfer?"

A "Oh dear!" shouted Grumio. "Afer isn't here, but here is our master Caecilius," the slave said **to the slave**.

"ēheu!" clāmāvit Grumiō. "Āfer abest, sed dominus Caecilius adest," (servum / servō) dīxit servus.

11.3 Which word does not belong?

1 Which word is *not* associated with "culīna"?

Circle the word that is out of place:

cēna

cibus

coquus

pāstor

pāvō

2 Which word is *not* associated with "theātrum"?

Circle the word that is out of place:

āctor

fābula

scaena

spectātōrēs

vīlla

3 Which word is *not* asssociated with "vēnālīcius"?

ancilla

nāvis

portus

servī

tuba

4 Which word is *not* associated with "versipellis"?

lupus

pulcher

silva

tunica

ululāvit

5 Which word is *not* associated with "cēna"?

bibit

cōnsūmit

lectus

tablīnum

triclīnium

6 Which word is *not* associated with "arēna"?

avārī

canēs

cervī

leōnēs

lupī

7 Which word is *not* associated with "basilica"?

accūsat

canis

cēra

iūdex

signum

8 Which word is *not* associated with "Graecī"?

barbarī

philosophī

pictōrēs

rhētorēs

sculptōrēs

11.4 What is the word?

Instructions: Fill the squares of the crossword puzzle with English words which have come to us from Latin.

Each word, numbered across or down, is clued below by (1) a related Latin word in parentheses and (2) a short English definition.

ACROSS

1 (*accipit*)   take
2 (*līberālis*) generous
4 (*inimīcus*) foe
5 (*canis*)   doglike

Continued

7	(*terret*)	frighten	20	(*parat*)	protective embankment
12	(*intellegit*)	clever	21	(*sentit*)	a feeling
14	(*celebrat*)	perform a ceremony	22	(*leō*)	carnivorous, tawny animal
17	(*terra*)	patio	23	(*ūnus*)	acrid vegetable of neatly-layered skins
19	(*domina*)	female equivalent of a knight	24	(*intrat*)	go in

DOWN

1	(*agit*)	representative, or person who has authority to act
3	(*incidit*)	definite, distinct occurrence; an event
6	(*īnspicit*)	examination
8	(*rēs*)	genuine
9	(*fugit*)	a runaway, or escapee
10	(*ad + nihil*)	reduce to nonexistence, or wipe out
11	(*reddit*)	give back what is proper
13	(*exspectat*)	consider likely
15	(*trādit*)	time-honored practice, or cultural custom
16	(*sedet*)	period of time devoted to a specific activity
18	(*rapit*)	forcible seizure of another's property

11.5 What is the meaning?

The words in the sentences below have been put in various orders which are new to you. Can you still translate the sentences? If you can, write a translation for each sentence on a separate sheet of paper.

1 servus quaerēbat gladium murmillōnī.
2 nārrāvērunt fābulam fīliīs fēminae.
3 rētiāriīs Rēgulus dedit signum.
4 mercātōrī dedit dēnāriōs fēmina.
5 spectāculum nūntiāvērunt cīvibus nūntiī.

Stage 12

12.1 Perfect-Tense Forms

1 *Instructions:* Whenever you are given a choice, circle the Latin verb-form in parentheses which is correct.

Caecilius sibi (dīxit / dīxī),

"ego cum Iūliō (cēnābam / cēnābat). subitō Clēmēns mihi rem tōtam (nārrāvit / nārrāvī). nōs omnēs urbem (petīvistis / petīvimus)."

Syphāx Caecilium (cōnspexit / cōnspexī) et (rogāvī / rogāvit),

"tūne uxōrem et fīlium (invēnit / invēnistī)?"

Caecilius Syphācī (respondī / respondit),

"ego Metellam et Quīntum nōn (invēnit / invēnī). ad vīllam meam nunc reveniō."

"tūne (vīdistī / vīdit) Clēmentem?" rogāvit Syphāx.

"ego (vīdī / vīdit)," respondit Caecilius. "Clēmēns cum Iūliō in templō (mānsit / mānsī)."

Continued

Caecilius virōs cōnspexit et rogāvit,

"vōsne familiam meam (vīdistis / vīdērunt)?"

virī (respondērunt / respondistis),

"nōs familiam tuam nōn (vīdērunt / vīdimus). num tū uxōrem tuam (āmīsistī / āmīsit)?" rogāvērunt.

Caecilius respondit,

"ēheu! ego Metellam (āmīsī / āmīsit). vōsne tremōrēs (sēnsistis / sēnsērunt)? vōsne sonōs (timēbant / timēbātis)? vōsne nūbem mīrābilem (cōnspexistis / cōnspexērunt)?"

virī nōn respondērunt, sed ē forō festīnāvērunt. Caecilius ad vīllam suam cucurrit.

2 On a separate sheet of paper, write a translation of the story above.

12.2 Perfect-Tense Forms

1 Write the number of each present-tense verb in column A in front of its perfect-tense equivalent in column B.

A	B	
1 abeō	____ sēnsī	_____
2 āmittō	____ exercuimus	_____
3 capiō	____ tacuimus	_____
4 damus	____ āmīsī	_____
5 exclāmō	____ revēnimus	_____
6 exercēmus	____ exclāmāvī	_____
7 īnspicimus	____ abiī	_____
8 revenīmus	____ dedimus	_____
9 sentiō	____ cēpī	_____
10 tacēmus	____ īnspeximus	_____

(*1st person sg. & pl. present*) (*1st person sg. & pl. perfect*)

A	B	
11 agitās	____ recubuistī	_____
12 cōnspicis	____ vēnistis	_____
13 cōnsūmis	____ scrīpsistis	_____
14 contenditis	____ cōnspexistī	_____
15 dūcis	____ cōnsūmpsistī	_____
16 necātis	____ contendistis	_____
17 petitis	____ agitāvistī	_____
18 recumbis	____ petīvistis	_____
19 scrībitis	____ dūxistī	_____
20 venītis	____ necāvistis	_____

(*2nd person sg. & pl. present*) (*2nd person sg. & pl. perfect*)

Continued

2 Write an English translation for each of the perfect-tense verbs in column B on the previous page, in the spaces provided.

12.3 Was Mt. St. Helens like Mt. Vesuvius?

On 18 May 1980, in the state of Washington, Mt. St. Helens erupted and has erupted several times since then less severely. An elderly lodgekeeper named Harry Truman died in the first eruption because he refused to leave when the warning tremors began.

This is a retelling of the story in Latin. First read the story and then, on a separate sheet of paper, write six comprehension questions in English which other students may answer. Can they?

mōns Sānctae Helenae

mōns Sānctae Helenae in Americā ōlim stābat pulcher et splendidus. mōns erat nōtissimus. multī hominēs ex urbibus discēdēbant et hunc montem vīsitābant. virī et fēminae per silvās ambulābant, et puerī et puellae ibi currēbant.

senex prope montem habitābat, ubi tabernam habēbat. senex fēlēs 5 amābat. multae fēlēs in tabernā hospitēs salūtābant et in mēnsās saliēbant.

subitō terra tremuit. senex et hospitēs sonōs ingentēs audīvērunt. hospitēs erant sollicitī.

"mōns est īrātus," inquit hospes.

"ego montem nōn timeō," respondit senex. "mōns est amīcus fidēlis. meus 10 mōns mē nōn terret."

iam nūbēs ātra ad terram dēscendēbat. iam cinis dēnsissimus incidēbat. hospitēs dēspērābant. hospitēs ad urbēs fūgērunt. senex tamen nōn dēspērābat. fēlēs nōn dēspērābant, sed latēbant et sē lambēbant.

postrīdiē fēlēs aberant. senex erat mortuus, mōns frāctus et sordidus. 15 īnfēlīx senex! mōns nōn erat amīcus fidēlis. mōns Sānctae Helenae erat alter Vesuvius.

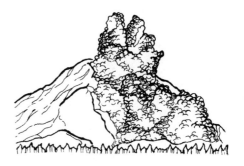

Progress Check

Stages 10–12

10 items × 10 points = 100 points

In each item, circle the Latin verb-form in parentheses that translates the **boldfaced** English words.

1 **I promised**
   (prōmīsī / prōmīsistī / prōmīsit)

2 **I was grabbing**
   (rapiēbās / rapiēbam / rapiēbat)

3 **you** (sg.) **were feeling**
   (sentiēbat / sentiēbam / sentiēbās)

4 **you** (pl.) **punched**
   (pulsāvimus / pulsāvistis / pulsāvērunt)

5 **we are inspecting**
   (īnspiciunt / īnspicimus / īnspicitis)

6 **you** (pl.) **are running away**
   (fugitis / fugiunt / fugimus)

7 **they invited**
   (invītāvistis / invītāvērunt / invītāvimus)

8 **I drank**
   (bibī / bibistī / bibit)

9 **they slept**
   (dormīvimus / dormīvērunt / dormīvistis)

10 **s/he frightened**
   (terruistī / terruit / terruī)